# Norman Weinstein

# NIGREDO

*Selected Poems 1970-1980*

## Station Hill

Station Hill Press, Barrytown, New York 12507.

Acknowledgements

Meshes 4 & 5" appeared in *Caterpillar* #20 (Clayton Eshleman, Editor, Sherman Oaks, Ca.)

"The Spanish Fandango" appeared in *Text* (Mark Karlins, Editor, New York, New York)

"A Dream of Origin" appeared in *Tree* #4 (David Meltzer, Editor, Bolinas, Ca.)

"Upstate Hunting: Ulster Gunning" & "Points on the Map" appeared in *Io* (Richard Grossinger, Plainfield, Vermont)

"The Uncertain Moralist" appeared in *Woodstock Poetry Review* (Pat Jackson, Editor, Woodstock, N.Y.)

"Elegy for Paul Blackburn" & "Meshes 7" appeared in *Sixpack* 7/8 (Pierre Joris & William Prescott, Editors, London & New York)

Drawings by Deborah Haynes

Produced at Open Studio in Rhinebeck, New York, a non-profit facility for independent publishers and individual artists, funded in part by grants from the New York State Council on the Arts and the National Endowment for the Arts.

**Library of Congress Cataloging in Publication Data**

Weinstein, Norman.
  Nigredo, selected poems, 1970-1980.

  I. Title.
PS3573.E3967N5        811'.54        82-7487
ISBN 0-930794-68-0                    AACR2

# NIGREDO: A SELECTION

**I**  *Interior Black*

**II**  *Black Sites*

**III**  *Portraits on Black*

for Clayton and Deborah
  whose care helped bring these poems to light.

# I  INTERIOR BLACK

# MESHES: 1

pockets of change to buy
exotic sweets almond marzipan
ambrosia sweet melon
less
change in my pockets
when "father" ceased functioning
as
evocation
table drawers filled with a diabetic's
nightmare lust
growing empty/
blood so sweet in both
parental bloodlines
"flies on a hot summer
day pick up our
scent a mile
away" trifles
as much
as Proust's teacake/
obvious sub
stitutions        that the
tongue of Learning
stay sweet
greatgrandfathers
poured honey in
to the willing open mouths of their
students
bringing them to the brink
of the mystery — Aleph
as if opening a virginal
labial lip
pressed w i d e/
A mother having to sleep alone for
a decade eating boxes of
cheap chocolates never
gaining a pound
A quarter gritty
gleaming in my palm
talisman
convertible to
a passing
glory say it this is the letter "A"
in sensation's
alphabet

                                        refusing these trinkets
        of cloying
                sweetness      called in
another text: "struggling
                        in the meshes
                                of samsara."

# MESHES: 2

her hand flexed
at her back, crab-
  like calling for me her
son swimming
 in city crowds shopping
    the Fantasy Stores
   where I'd be
exchanged for another
      child
    who'd please
her Husband more
  driving for fast
   value prodding
 for muscle
& raw
      brute presence
  I lost in his
 affections
      like a moon/struck
  country girl
her first
      night
         in the hay
& he wishing
for a son to assume
   the Fantasy business
  her hand gasping at her back carrying me
      from his ideal
    but still
  considering bringing
      me for trade-in

## MESHES: 3

somewhere in a grey Philadelphia
afternoon as you
skim this page
a neon sign with the word: W E I N S T E I N
flickers
off/on in roughly
pulse rhythm
& as it flickers
a neon
hammer is hitting
a neon nail on the head sending it
into a hauntingly
lit plank
& in a blink
the action repeats: the nail
miraculously raises itself
from the plank &
gets driven down
again

next to this the word: H A R D W A R E
out of order

like the warrior's
shield in the Iliad
in micro
cosm my entire

tribal history
fate
first

illumination

# MESHES: 4

"anyway you cut the deck . . ."
& he wasn't referring
to a hand of blackjack or Tarot
but to all the choices a man
might make to sustain
a marriage & sounded remote,
abstract in his determinations.
his hand tapping a gold shot glass
in a bar 12 blocks from
where he would return me after visiting
hours. Each card dealt pressing an
impossible choice upon him. The
Joker covering the Queen. Edging
for the image of himself —faded King —
in his son but the Queen
imposing & she who divides the
spoils of the game? war? done/ he
turned the glass upsidedown watching
ale uselessly spill on
formica. Gone. A second
after the game's
over everyone's glued in their
seats waiting for the tables
to be cleared. Never are. Some tokens
of the losers — half lit cigarettes, match
covers, cracked chips left behind. Souvenirs
of a deadend life. He's the
man who even with a deck of aces
would come off losing & this his
source of wisdom: a shot glass righted
before paying: its entire
contents: what he believed about
the weaker
sex

## MESHES: 5

those pin-up
            girl calendars
      my father
    gave to clients
            lifting
    cellulose sheet
    to glance at the
          breasts

      then

      finish the sale

## MESHES: 6    contents of my father's wallet

which when you splay the leather mouth opens
corresponds in shape
to bladder,
prostate,
lung chamber,
heart.

come midnight a team of surgeons wheels the old
man into O.R. for the
burlesque. Like old strippers
they peel layer after
layer of ulcerating tissue away, fill
hollowed out organ pockets
with monopoly money. Play
cash hurts no body & opaques

in x-rays as real.

screened fine enough so
the words gel under low
magnification

old lies about "TRUST"

& a "him" a wrathful
motherfucker

with an urge

to cut

any feminine-looking
organ

          OUT
by its bloody
roots

## MESHES: 7

there were "bad men"
        hanging out late in
    dim lit
    tap-rooms
in dense cigarette atmosphere
      talking
loudly,
       obscenely,
spending
recklessly
        returning
  home
slurred
& vague


      some, "like diamonds
in the rough" their women
put up with their
ex
  girlfriends & wallets
I suppose those sad sad songs
of the 30's said it all
I was born later
      at 6 brought
into the bar, sat
on a stool at the confused
  rings of lights
  the loud
      assertions
   the towering
faces too
     close
 breathing, was told later
  raised hell crying
until taken
home  the good men sleep in
   the good men
embracing wives
   emptying wallets for clothes bread mortgage
        the good women giving their tired flesh to
them   /but coveting their
   first romances
  there's the door reading: WOMEN ONLY
I thought of (sadly) finding in an old text the words
    "angels of women's paradise" where
  the good men go
after work

## MESHES: 8

                shattered back/
                        bone
           of the men
   who were father grand
                fathers
           to me
   Ezekial's boneyard backyard shattered
                father out the door
           impotence
   in their lack
   of solidness
                the women their wives planted
                *their* homes &
   laughing at their men
                push-overs,
   sitting huddled over their soup, tauted
                "where's your BACKbone?"
           & he slammed the door the front
   entrance is he coming
                back
   the pain at the base of his spine
                an inheritance
           (what can I relate
   to their sex
                lives I imagine
      collapsing into bed after
                work flat
           on his back
   after Pearl Harbor
      "a new born babe — helpless"
           my back
   is all the definition
                        of my past
           I maintain
   its hard curve
           curled
      to my
   touch    /carapace
           cat-toughness
      raised in anger, armor
      against the women
   who have tested
                its presence
           Ezekiel facing his skeleton a voice saying your father
                        is gone
                & you're the man

17

        of the house
"Stand
up"
        & sensation of being pushed from behind
        her hands on my spine
back break

## MESHES: 9

      screening
           throwing my face
into stark relief

          ·    a voice dictated:
     "You may speak to your father but not for more than a moment"
   Remembered
           Odysseus
                 addressing the shadow
            force of his mother. How
              bathed in longing,
                words dropped like spears in an ill
                fated wind
                  an Orphic lament guilt-laced

                                   asked
Him if the wire mesh cutting
us off from each
other might be
removed he
gestured as if to signal
such factors
were beyond his comprehension
                    or control.

                         His breath
          irregular & labored thru the screening
          said blindly
thankgod you're still well

             "I've been sick since
                   you were born"
   focusing
each area of his face, fallen
cheeks, dead
tension lines at his eyes

            a lithograph the reversal of which
            reveals: a Life-Source souring
            in his father's genes, runaway from
            Czarist army only to turn into
            military-rigid overLord
            (one moment — the dictation
returned)

a feminine voice said: I can not grant more)

brought my face
as near as the screen permitted my lips against his

"you long
for who I never was"

When the screens went on the first summer days I acted
as if I were being sealed in a chamber, a Poe-like
restraining barrier. Bounding to get: out: anywhere. He would arrive,
& in his largesse toss me over his shoulders say we're going out
for the day & the front door screen
OPENS

"IF YOU LEAVE WITH HIM DON'T COME BACK!"

"across dangerous territory"
in the back of his Ford pick-up, bars
on the back window
"I'm keeping you out of trouble" he laughs
rocky suspension on those cobblestone by the dock streets
real steel
I touch my hands to the cold disbelieving
holding on as the truck lurches
10, 15 years
I get off

His hand turns away from the screen
pained/
futile to throw his strength across
the table to reach me

the uncompleted lithograph
(memory
dictates this entire life will complete if necessary

"You may touch his face

can't harm you anymore"

## MESHES: 10   Mara Tantra

brittle as tinsel
mara actual first love

& pure "image" initial
hieroglyph of what woman is   a dish

filled with grains from
parental honeymoon snap

shot & movie & romantic
novel femme fatale

             to escape her grip:

   throwing
    her to the ground
pinning her down with
     one knee
   smallness of her
   that I feel rage at raping
    doll, char-
acter − − −, she is
   NOT
that she struggles at my throat draws
    blood
   from my lips

  pulls me to
   her breasts
 undisguised
    thru her blouse
   tosses me whirls
    me circling
      her
    circling
    groggy, some of the rage
       leaking
   out at last
   she is lying in slip &
      bra
 serpentine
     I am loathe
  to meet her here

  snake coiling tightening around
      Mara-imago

Maximus tale of woman siphoning
                              off snake venom
taste
        of her snaking tongue
                        touching mine shut
            to memory
                    look at her shadow
                        crossing my life in the poem
                                from that corner of my mouth she reached
                        kissing nervously
                        begin to speak
                        words stop


                                sweating, bending
                                        over her
thighs, a spoke
      of light
    from a passing
              car crossing
them as I enter


                her, then
                        STOPPED
        she said stop I want a
        FAMILY! &
        with that word evoked father
                    pulling maternal
                    pulling puppet FAMILY
            show for a children's cardboard
                        box stagefront, I


            collapsed
                        on her breasts, pulling
at her nipples      wanting to meet her at
                        that
                        junction
                                unshielded
                came there, angrily, un
                        released my in
                    visible family
            spasmed in my veins at
                                my heart re
                reminding me their presence


            pulls me toward that
            field of imagination where

                                    true mother
                                                father
          are sought

meditating on the many-headed
angel whose
left hand leads me
to praise mara, whose
right leads me

to grab her chin & force
utterance

get out those lying words
her father's
father planted:

F A M I L Y  L O V E

## MESHES: 11

barbed wire & screens
divided the Adult book
store like Berlin
like an Irving Berlin song
"Foot loose & fancy
free"? climbed
over make
shift barrier
& mother was knitting
in a dark lit corner
hanging above her
grey skull: a copy of TEEN
MASTURBATION FANTASY,
a tattered German paper
back of *Thus Spake
Zarathustra* & a 45
of Bob Willis & the Texas
Playboys singing "The
Spanish Fandango" Rock-
abilly blaring thru con
cealed ceiling speakers
cashbox in front stuttered
To cross from the front
door to the rear screened
section is to drop adolescent
intensities & romances &
as you rip the cellophane off
TEEN FANTASY its pages liquefy
at air touch return to pulp
& petroleum viscous semen strands
run off your fingers & an arab
boys offers you a good time cheap
but mother's sitting knitting for you

a codpiece
adorned with
bloodred roses
with real
wire stems to

plant in your pulsebeat

# MESHES: 12

her name isn't goddess her
name is Blackman, Weinstein,
Meltzer, Gold. Many
marriages. & like Adam
in Paradise I
name the strange beasts
manifested by each
I do. I do? I do
want to open a trap door
& let my genealogy fall out
of my asshole? Not
an ungrateful
son. Here, mother. A word
necklace for
solace & rosary
to keep you entertained
while I run out the door.
I'm 18 & 18 & when
I finish I'll retire. Knock
against my spine. Hands of a
Japanese healer hitting pressure
points says: like some
body hit your back with
a hammer. Anyone home? Fire/goddess
with loud nag for an anvil. Hitting
animusbone with tales
of missing father. Yet mercy
compels a broader vision: her
loneliness & myself as poor
companion, too
tiny to crawl under sheets to satisfy
her. Strike
those lines. Don't. Keep
faithful to pain's
emergent form. Father's
lumpen clay blob out
of family kiln
she strikes him —BAM!— &
his pieces get stuck
in my kidneys throat nose
any one piece contains whole pot
bending myself around the wheel
throwing my sick flesh into shaping
this poem from
clay sifted
thru fine wire mesh
the pebble like memories of missing affection

# THE DEAD CHILD

1.

in the artist's abdomen cooks
a dense plasmic broth I name:
"the dead child" a stillborn
soul state existing in an un
ceasing imbalance between
imaginative force & surrender
to the parental hemmed-in vision—
every deep breath intake activates
the dead child, wakes him
to a setting as alien
as Blake found literal London
in an American city in the Sixties

the dead child finds himself riding
the gleaming copper coaches of
*The Psychoanalytical Express.* Every
other rider's creased face treated
by an absolute Freudian. The dead child kills
time on this ride comparing his sickness
to Scriabin's, who invented
a contraption to strengthen his piano
playing fingers. Whole mechanism
crushed his entire right hand. Then
took to composing Etudes for
Left Hand only. The dead
child realizes: this is my self pulled
toward women with hearts cocked
as guillotines. After every abortive
affair a bit of my anatomy
gets severed, new
loves—improvisations
created from my intact
bones.
        who's
the actual analyst informing
this writing? Remember M. who
held my blown/apart anatomy
in his arms while I shivered that my dead
child wouldn't survive $50
an hour. Cheap

babysitting keeping the dead
child underground, between stops, out

of his mother's dreams

2.

in a world where imagination
gets reduced to caprice or
escape, unreality, the dead child

finds in the heft
& weight of words solace &
a probe to sound the real. A Physician

from a Homeric age & blind visits
in a dream & is oracular: *"Treat
yourself in this world like*

*a hemophiliac forced to take
a night's lodging on a bed
of nails. Don't*

*stir in your dream.* An order to
honor fragility? Impossible since
my words pull me into dangerous

terrain. Then injunction to live
with vision's circumference
attentively. A child carrying

in its palm a soap bubble. A
dead child carrying in its
soul crudely carved images

of its origins: branching poplar—
menorah—fetal nerve
bundle—father's massive

fist—
mother's broken
jaw

# THE SPANISH FANDANGO

With fan flurry & eyes
she hid herself from her suitors
light in the dance hall
a gelatin red like her

lips & rouge. Atmosphere
cloudy as ether, penetrating
caused the exit signs to glow
—amulets in a medieval love

allegory. Mother reached in her
compact & saw her image expand
within the limits of a tortoiseshell
mirror. Then contract/ To the size of

*as mother you can't flirt with fathers*
Closes her image, accepts the
persistent man with a diamond
on each finger. They whirl in dream

time. Hours pass in seconds. Her
heart keeping time like a paper
fan. Whatever life is, she thinks, this
swirling holding her gently is height

& from her shaking tower she holds this man
in her arms as married child. The dance
accelerates in her mind, her fingers
webs of a fan hiding the dreariness of the

dance hall from her glowing vision. That
corny fandango music causes her
to trip over her gown. Goodnaturedly she
lifts her skirts. Denied suitors look away. The

music ceases. A melodic divorce. The man
in her arms dissolves like cigarette
ash. Standing pretty & alone in stage
center closes her fans & calls for her

son 30 years away writing the poem to
keep her company until the dance hall empties.
He hears her but sees her companion returning
to her arms hiding his face behind a fan

his blurred profile kissing hers as the dreadful
music roars to finale & Spanish music means
songs of civil discord & reunion
rouge of middleage & spriteliness

of the bitter chase

# THE SPANISH FANDANGO: 2

When Lorca saw the fandango danced at Columbia
A student farce & rite of passage
young breasts crushed like dayold carnations
stiff ramrod male shoulders thrusting for home
he

for a fleeting second
not Spanish not American
learned the yoga of satisfaction
*I want & I want*
Uncatholic
the girls of the 30's class
thought him

boyish
A church bazaar stuffed doll of an
artist
to sleep with under
their pillows
Don't blame the music

or the writer
his poems unread making
a jackass of himself on the thrashing
floor

with exaggerated
florid steps he
laughed at his own
ungainliness. The fandango

became unfashionable
before he finished the dance. Susan
Duende, then 42, now 18, remembers
him as a poor fandango partner. Hitler

loved to watch
other men dance with his mistress
the fandango. At Columbia a janitor recalls
how the odor of castile lingered in

the gymnasium. He himself carried Lorca
into a waiting taxi. Holding the door open
for the unconscious. Writer. Arm stiff &
unyielding as a fandango master

The dance to keep one's armor tight.

# THE SPANISH FANDANGO: 3

the naked teenagers feigning disinterest
at the end of a long island afternoon
sit smoking tapping their cigarettes
in time to the radio newscast rhythm
their eyes cool & anxious waiting for
the right set of coincidences for a pick
up stare with admiration at their tanned
limbs. The radio crackles like a jealous
father. Faces of exquisite boredom Renoir
knew enough to find in every young woman's
face among his people. They shed their towels
& gingerly run across the sand into the chilling
waters. Every male eye on the beach sizes them
up. The water rises to their hips. Their breasts
are wonderfully young. Stupidly they joke
with one another as the waves carry them further out
of my range of vision. Rocking like buoys they stand
passive as the waves cover them. They do nothing for
the willing admiration of the eyes on the shore
except offer their images. Brashly. This appeals. This
is the exhibitionism of the artist or idiot. & their
audience —myself— we sit on the dunes eyes dancing
in our heads a dance, any dance, a fandango
with an entire ocean to veil their steps

# THE SPANISH FANDANGO: 4

A transparent
bodysuit should
be worn to dance
the fandango a zipper
from throat hollow
to base of genitals with
easy single fluid motion
the body opens like a
pomegranate the flesh ruddy
& with a stinging sweetness
with American frenzy
& middleclass abandon
with Psyche's fury
& eros' drivenness
you learn to unzipper
the flesh seam, look
into chest center & see
light particles dance
rainbow-spectrumed blood
& arctic reefs of bone &
you know by now the last true
physician's an alchemist
fires under his alembic
well tended dancing the fandango
his laboratory ransacked for being
accurate the master himself
hung for dancing the fandango as one
continuous
movement of copulation

# THE SPANISH FANDANGO: 5

Imagine a foolish artist thrashing on his analyst's
couch — or sleeping in a marriage

bed as reprieve. A Hanged
Man's a master of several

steps. My father
hanging himself from a garage

rafter, asks me, 6, to
tap dance, un

coordinated, un
syncopated foxtrot, a

ridiculous clown who
won't let me touch

his hanging knot
tho the ceiling rafter yields

Sputters: "Your mother *drove* me"
brushes sawdust from his pants &

goes out for a drink. Years pass.
The garage collapses like a house

of cards, the Hanged Man, the last
card falls laterally a fetus/man kicking

through a birth canal. Vertically remember
seeing under his free floating legs every

possible (deal of the deck) dance but
his wife's favorite — but a man & his

suicide were never partners
for the fandango

# THE SPANISH FANDANGO: 6

ten years to learn
to enter the life
of a city is to grasp
the proper manner the path
of knowing how to travel its
streets without losing your own
body outline. Literally the soul
who walks Manhattan as it would
Lenox loses its body. Is re
turned in the form of an
overstuffed cardboard suitcase
waiting like death in a bus terminal
locker. The city walk is
crude, ungentle, appropriate.
Is highstepping. Is hell for the neck
& shoulders. Is the same for the dead
& insane.                    Think of that
dated ballroom dance: the fandango.
                    Think how many shot
gun marriages were triggered by its
hyperbolic gestures. Why walk any city
except to find your lover & build a single
life outside
of the city limits
where the fandango as well as the French tango
are forbidden
in public places
after dark.

# 3 OF CUPS CARD EXPLAINED

A year since I had slept
with anyone. I go
to a bar & sit & meditate
on how the smoke rises
like the cost of one minute
of honest sex. I don't drink.
I watch. The King of Soul
dances with the Queen
of Spades. An atmosphere
like the day after Mardi Gras
permeates the room. I don't want
a minute of honest sex, want
a lifetime. Finally, as I'm
about to leave a middleaged
Italian woman, plump, dressed
like a gypsy asks if she
can join me. Slides next
to me before I can answer. Starts
the usual patter: politics &
power & evidently she's
telling me NOBODY can satisfy
her in bed but...I can try. I
can't. The Queen of Spades'
shoulders flash by me as
straps of her dress loosen.

Because I want a life
I listen to this woman's longing
as if she's performing a
power gathering ritual. She is.
Sucking energy from my groin &
leaving me with a tablecloth
of ashes. The eternal triangle.
The gypsy, myself & my longing

join hands & drunkenly shuffle
across the floor & when her wig
slips during our steps know she's

not even a woman & beneath the gaiety
of this card under epicene gowns

pretty boys praise the May pole & I
fear being asked to join the circle

# AUNT

Married young to a gambler.
Too many bad days
at the races. Told
me every man has his

vices. Lost his week's
earnings. Told
to move out. Did she hint
he drank? Stunk of 4

roses, cheap havanas? No man's
perfect. Rinsed her hair
carrot red. Dressed smartly.
Never remarried. Told me she's

without regrets. Lives in
working class Baltimore. Doesn't
hate (she claims) anything
but niggers. No safety walking

bleak night avenues.
"Take care of your mother" she
holding my wrist insisted. "She
NEEDS you" Rough ride in packed

pullman cars to Philly. Jewish
for the high holidays. Her true
religion lurking behind every
street corner satanic figures: men,

men,
they'll-go-out-&-blow-
your-last-dime-
men.

# A DREAM OF ORIGIN

a wooden child's
block with Hebrew lettering. Aleph

spoke facing me: "only I'm
ultimately responsible for your

actions." I began
to argue the block vanished

reappeared in the fireplace its
letters luminous going up with the smoke

I want to tell that *I* was re-
sponsible flames engulfed my

house the fireplace was left
burning in open air around a

shattered houseframe burning like
Adam's lips after saying the first

word —
the pain of not letting wood speak

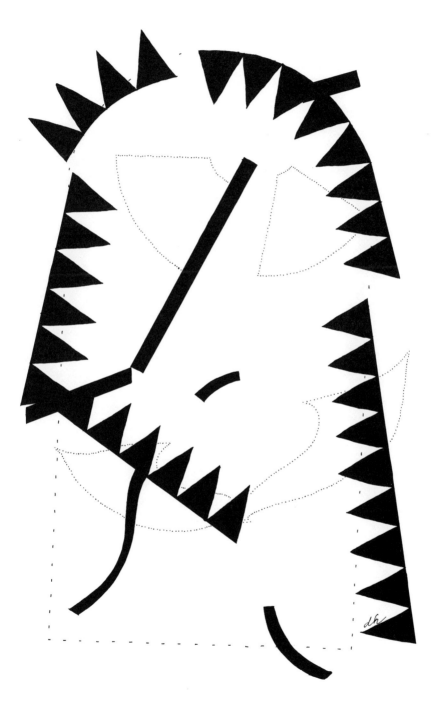

sleep penetrates me the way timelessness
penetrates a Navaho sand painting depicting: a crow
giving birth to the earth. This my first
night's sleep on Laguna's sand. A dream
yields this image: the gull who invented California.
A winged gatherer of discarded fragments, cubist collagist,
like the poet dreaming on an otherwise empty beach listening
in his dream to the soft scratchings of gulls watching
receding shoreline. The gull draws runes
in the sand signifying its intentions: if I'll read its
cards, it'll tell, in runic rhyme, California's fate.
Meanwhile: a naked Pomo woman runs past us holding a
small turtle against her crushed breasts. The sun's
risen 6 times 5 as a diamond sixth as an ale cup. The
crow of the sand painting hangs in the sky: a day constellation.
The gull grows impatient with these distractions, I cut
the deck, rest the spread on a beach blanket & show: a
dominance of swords & cups. As I'm about to narrate
these cards, a radio finds its voice: a 50s ballad, teenage
lover killed on train tracks, her grieving boyfriend
slits his wrists joining her in radio paradise. I
scream over the lyrics: YOUR NATURE IS TO PICK AT YOUR
LOVE TO GET TO THE QUICK OF HER LEAVING YOU COLD HERES
TIME TO LEARN TO FIND A CALM SECOND WITH HER NOT
STRUTTING BUT SOARING ALONGSIDE HER GLIDE. After I'm
finished the gull suddenly jumps in the midst of the cards,
uses its feathers like pistons, scatters the spread, sends
cards flying into an approaching wave. Draws a square
walking a perfect box figure. Flies to the wave's edge,
pecks, dives for a card catching it in its beak, flies
back to the box outlined in the sand, deposits the card
in its center. The card: the Fool. Before I find time
to ask its meaning, a wave slams, full impact, destroys
either California or myself. Leaves one of us behind
to tell this.

# UPSTATE HUNTING: ULSTER GUNNING

inbreath  :  entire
side of Bear Mountain
wearing its coat
its mink cape dotted with blood
hunters
in atomic
sleighs
image/lusters
when faced with actual
bear turn away
violently it isn't dark flesh
they hunger secretly for
the stinking bulk of bear
carcass wearies
their seeing. They're
finding
their manhood: a key
jammed in an
accelerator, a car
swerving off the road
past a guard rail into
a side of bear &
the bear's blood
brings the sky to an
overhanging damp
climax, the clouded
sun is
a tangle of burst
arteries giving
the cold light
of the dying

\*    \*    \*

outbreath:

remote tele
phone of a warbler
                    definite
report
of a Remington, branch
flies into
            my windshield

I pick
up the receiver

blood runs down
the length
of my
sleeve

## ANNANDALE SPRING 69

*for David Abel*

into the worst torrential
(the angel of action interrupts: "resist description")
lightning thunder booms cold rain
into which two naked women
running from their dorm
                                        shouts,
arms raised, running to the Hudson
& back
(you're hooked into that image
of their sensuality, pass beyond it the
dictation insists)

but their long hair
matted against
their heaving breasts

*pothos, pathos —*

why they dared the storm?
my unresolved longing for their
courage?
their crazy naked end of the 60s
put on?

besides the point

where their image
lives
a house of nothing
but doorways is

going up, don't

mistake this for
nostalgia, it's
all the home we'll ever know

& whoever knocks doesn't
stop as long as we
write

## APPALACHIAN SPRING
## THE THEME FROM

they come after 25 years out
of the mines with half
a lung, weak vision &
a cripple's gait

at 40 good enough to
spend the day on a back
porch with a banjo &
fiddle & a Jug & play precise

bluegrass til sundown. A
glossy postcard to send
the folks up North except
when Don & his brother

Fred put on white sheets
& terrorize the town's
one black family. They make
a raspy grating throaty sound

ghostly when they're on
the attack. Leave to sociology
their motives. I hear
an extension of their back

porch music. In its rhythms
their souls get in
cubated. Psyche assumes
linen wings & flies like a

suicidal moth thru the
fires of a burning cross. Notes
spring out of the raped
earth & drive our friends

into that rapture even
the old Greeks trembled
to ponder the consequences
of

# OUTSIDE MILL CREEK, WEST VIRGINIA, 1973

high voltage fires glowing
thru oak tree root work. A West
Virginia pasture defined
toward the East by a cow
pasture toward the West by a
clapboard frontier church where
a sacramental snake gets passed
among the sunday devout. Lazy
in white noon heat black guernseys
piss into clumps of warm weeds. A stirring
slippery motion at boot heels — a snake
coiling in suspended animation then

clarity of no-fear ——
finger on my camera shutter:
TIME EXPOSURE

make it last
at least one

lifetime.

# HARRISBURG

from out of the whirlwind
of Black Elk's broken
hearted vision of defeat

at the hands of the heart
less Whites, from out of
Wovoka's prophetic hat & Crazy

Horse's final ecstasy, clear
how red guardians of earth
& pure stream had to be murdered.

Clear how the Whites had a passionate
affair with slow poisoning &
poisoning their children marks

only the start of their death/dance.
No ghost dancers needed to avenge
tribal honor. Simply: a water valve,

an engineer's broken nerve & in
visible bison stampede thru
Pennsylvania darkness trample silently

already sick genes
of the already dead
race.

## OAKLAND GUNS

inner city pawn shop
you go thru 2
wire mesh electronically
controlled doors
confront the owner
with a 45 strapped across
his beerbelly
& if you're a leading
citizen get
led into the
back room
to see the special
collection. as the owner
closes shop he
stares in every direction
as he locks the next to
last then front
door & then walks
into the unsafe
streets where

a truck from the
San Andreas coffin company

damn near kills him.

# OAKLAND SOUND

a time of life when the old gods
                                & goddesses
       give up in
               habiting worn
                      flesh
of the bodies walking downtown Oakland.
                                    Nobility
           no longer specific
       to how their broadrimmed hats perch how their
                                 hips
                                     sway
Praise to the soul carrying his cassette recorder roaring
           forcing private static
               in his skull
                      into public
    gesture. & tho the gods
                     are FINISHED with his
         ale/drenched liver & blood
                              shot eyes
at remove they delight in his booming sound
                             trumpeting
            past the welfare building
                      loud as Zeus
               fare
                  thee
                    well

## URBAN RENEWAL

on a hill over
looking the only un
developed hill left in
San Francisco where some
fool is trying to
put up a condominium
we lean against a half
completed house frame, caress
& let our hands roam
under our clothes &
surprised by your
sudden public passion wonder

what provoked you? Images
of the collapse of
our fantasy nation?

Knowing
in your marrow the
only holy city
we can inhabit

remains flesh
the planners cant box
in
yet

# WILL YOU LIVE TO SEE PARADISE?

"WILL YOU LIVE TO SEE PARADISE?" asks
the *Watchtower* newspaper headline
in the tight

fisted grip of the wrestler
turned evangelist
in front of the drug store

making no sales pitch.
It's california & paradise
rents you know where &

for what.
Or do I know?
Lead ink from his hot palm

running riot in his head.
The day an oppressive
white heat with smog

at eye level. A middle
aged woman in low cut mumu
runs screaming into avenue

traffic in
terrogating random drivers:
"DO YOU KNOW WHERE THE RAIN COMES FROM?"

Apparently they don't they
drive on
if not to Paradise at least

Los Angeles.
Melodramatic she beats her
breast. A siren snakes

into shrillness. The
Mental Hygiene Dept. gets
a new test subject knowing

no rain falls in Paradise.
No one need wait
to see it. It's

as plain as a headline.
Feel the newspaper vendor's
nervousness as the cop

51

cars pull up to take her
away. Thinking he's next?
Perhaps myself crazy to believe

this IS paradise &
hell's where the old news
papers proclaiming apocalypse

go up in smoke

# GOLETA

by the phoenix-constant light
of the derricks a pale

stallion out of
Ryder gallops toward

shore
oil sticking to its hoofs

careful
it doesn't crush you to death

on its backside branded
its name: "FOLLY

OF INDUSTRY" or if
that's too apparent try

"UPPITY URIZEN"
when it neighs

lights go off
all over downtown Santa

Barbara when it
sleeps 4

children contract
leukemia

when it angers
a glass of city water

kills in minutes

# WINNEMUCA, NEVADA

coyote told bear-child:

this is where the White Devils
believed they found
entrance to the bowels
of the earth/ Note

how the layout
of the city most
resembles a human
anus prepared
to expel gas. & how
its citizens are mainly
gas &
water held together
by this fiction they call
"tourist bucks."   .   Don't

you find
this concept
of place rather
bizarre, bear-child?


                    bear-child
scratched its furry head
& replied:

Not at all, coyote
brother. I have heard
in the White Devil's
Scripture that when

Apocalypse comes
thousands of citizens
will flee California
& arrive, panting, credit
cards in hand at these
motels & filling stations

eventually, they will
find the accommodations
wanting & build cities
underground

coming into the dusty air
once a year
for a rodeo or
funeral or

a trip to the bank

# POINTS ON THE MAP

there are
currents of
energy hid

under ground that

drive the needle of
a compass to point
anywhere
but north

but who with
the courage to toss
a compass to the ground
& follow

its leanings to Hell if need be?

the corpse
of Mishima & with him his glittering boys

rigid

pointing
(anywhere

but due
North

# BLOCKED EXIT

the stench of emptying bus
terminals; flickerings
of overhead
fixtures at airports after
midnight; abandoned
benches of pennsylvania
station; dense
granular air of the customs
booth at the Mexican
border; houses
of friends forgotten
over a decade; form
lessness of their parent's
formalities; because

of these locations
I will never never
never
learn the ritual
of leaving
cleanly what
must leave me

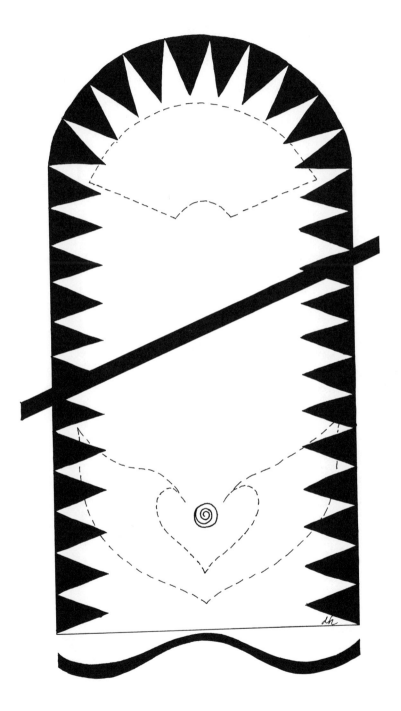

# THE UNCERTAIN MORALIST

A Russian Jew tailor with his little
death perched inside his top/hat
which he would never remove
entering a stranger's house, a
center of his actual anatomy
wanting to be buried with it
(demanding his wife do so)
like a phantom limb any
injury to his top/hat a
blow to his heart
*the hat is a protector*
he told me (related
by the vaguest of blood
lines) *when*
*you take it off*
*at the wrong*
*time or place your*
*death sizes up*
*your body &*
*decides how*
*best to*
*finish it off*
But once
I saw him thoughtless
tip his hat
so very slightly
to a youngwoman emerging
from the subway he
could never have known
beauty being (unspoken) the
sole possible
exception to his rule

# CAN YOU SCRATCH MY HEART?

The first three sections of this poem are verbatim transcriptions drawn from the words of a migrant worker fortune declared I would share a bench & bus trip with in New York in 1972. This poem is given with pleasure to the man whose words inform the opening sections & the title is his.)

1.

she used to be
    tellin me
all the time I
   love
yous baby I
   love
yous I
  love
    you
     & I said
to her I
  said —
    BABY
Can you
  scratch
    my heart?
      She said
what you
  talkin
    bout?
I said
  Can you scratch
    my heart?

        Well,
she said
  nothing to that & to
      this day
I aint seen
  her

   again

2.

you know
the biggest pro
missory note they make is this here
50,000
dollar bill
&
let me tell
you some
thin
that bill
aint worth as much
as one
drop of
your blood
I told this
to this dude
on the street
man &
he says
why I'd
bash your
head in
for 10
bucks
you ever see
one of them
bills its
got Woodrow
Wilson on
it but it
aint worth
as much
as one drop
of your
blood

3.

all my relatives
they all dead
but 2
they all died
on their
knees
praying
I aint
gonna pray
to *their*
god I mean
the man who
pays & puts
vittals in my
house he's the
god I should
pray & say grace
to you
see what I
mean they go
& hear preachin
til that preacher
shouts til the veins
stick out behind
his ears hollerin
& screamin but the man
who pays me &
I get vittals from
when I sit
down at the table
I don't say
dear lord
I say thank you
mr. cornpone
or miss ratoff
or whoever for
puttin food
in my belly & that
man's my god I know
one thing mister I ain't
dying like they
did

on my knees.

4.

a store confronts you on your path
in dream-time no
identifying signs
you enter the store
has the dimensionality
of soul no
imperatives
but to SEE
each wall lined
with glass cabinets
rising to the ceiling
each cabinet lined
with darkwood shelves
purple velvet covering
on each shelf displays
of fine jewels in settings
& unpolished crude stones
earth stained
as you stand admiring
a salesman approaches
asks you your interest
as you fumble silently
he reaches into his suit pocket
withdraws a fist & opens
each petal like finger
to reveal: a dozen tiny jade
hearts riding ridges
of his palm's creases
telling both his heart
breaks & your own he

tosses the hearts abruptly
in the air then bends
& scoops them off the
green carpet with a
flourish

unscratched

for a price you can have
initials scratched
on their surfaces

the store lights dim
as I replay the scene, the circus
beauty of the hearts juggled

my desire to grab them
out of the dream air a
fantasy stopped

by a loud pulsing chime
the salesman's hurried
explanation of how he
must lock the displays

store walls expanding/
contracting with each chiming

a hand thrusts out
behind a display case
opening a dictionary to
"jade" where

two meanings merge:
the precious stone, &

a vicious woman. & sensing

my heart's history
written with both
meanings in mind

5.

found in the Hasidic
lore a
        willingness
to live out

            the Fool

                    a divine
calling to permit
heart
        to be scratched
                        over
& over

            sorting out
            old love poems
            to toss in a fire

calling forth images &
under
each image

                Helen
                Eve
                Lilith

the record of my not unique
romantic follies
typical of my
age &
situation

            but noting
            the poems opening
            the heart
            gate

those armoring

"there is a dragon
blocking access to the fountain
of life" an old
Arab text records
                & my task in these
measures:
            scratching
                    the dragon's
                            heart?

# THE HISTORY OF VOODOO

: that elegant white specter
Maya Deren
Hunter College alumna tracking voodoo demons in 16mm
An oldwoman riding the train with me says of her:
"I remember her when her name was..."

& how I've never
tolerated
such talk echos in
my ears like a field recording of a Southern chain gang

the moon
(refusing to be cast in her film)
asks a question of blood
a demon stopped up in a sherry bottle
catches in its glass face pearl teeth
of the moon
& a phonograph reciting Dixieland

the needle caught at crescendo

I honor that nervously
excitable lost woman finding her spirit's
shape actual Haiti with fires

sporadically
bringing the left hand not to know
the business
of the right

       the spirit
dances where
it may
    Finds
focus where the cold
moon glare
       is a pool of
blood, the
question is never whose but
when &
finally

the ritual
dictates: *the place of your rebirth*
*your altar site must*
*be circumambulated (nightly)* I am

reborn in the film
of Maya Deren's eyes, the film
locked in a closet 20 years after her death for "personal reasons"
too painful to be told
how she caught the natives (myself) with blood singeing their lids

Spooks
who (on film) (when their demons were stopped up in wine bottles)
whirling found flesh they believed was dead or yet to be born.

# THE SECRET LIFE OF SIDNEY BECHET

"Jung is my nemesis" said Sidney
as the stage lights inflame
his vision. Keeps mis
taking women hanging a-
round his act for women — rather
than lizards. Made love
to their
scales playing fractured
modal scales. Better
than suicide or a
bad fuck
or smoke. When you breathe
out in
to your horn, his Creole teacher
taught your
unconsciousness
is brought to a fine point, the
eye of a
storm or nerve.
He remembered, christ,
their pearl white teeth were
inhuman, crack
biting down to play
Cole Porter bleeding at the belly

2.

a particular juncture
of life when a few running
scales on sax or piano
evoke 1934 Berlin a torrent
of dire decadence &
Sidney is a jew
& I'm a jew asked
to play for Hitler
Hitler who thinks
all jazz is Negro copulation
blues. Sidney plays march
music instead, Stravinsky
's parody of a tin
soldier's march Hitler
isn't amused Sidney
deadpans calls his final
number: "Uncircumsized Soul"
At least, thinks Hitler, here
is a man not afraid of being
modern

3.

listening to a car tape while you aborted
some archive collection
your fetus isn't Sidney
weaves in & out of un
distinguished combinations. The gas
left you groggy like
a sax solo reverberating
through a subway tunnel. Old mistresses
you had long forgotten, Sidney, come
to let bygones be etc. You run to
the exit steps but
your leg muscle spasms. Like
a swallowed note. An aborted take. The
subway platform won't hold the crowds
of your forgotten lovers. Some
men dressed like society
bitches. How full the world
is of overripe admiration you think when
all you want is
*will you stop me from trembling*
*in my sleep?*

4.

The Hanged Man's an instrument new to jazz
if Jesus had hung inverted
jazz would have been created

imagines Sidney, rejecting suicide.

5.

Walking down the staccato white line
center strip of the Santa
Monica Freeway the white line
blackens as his steps approach
his soles smearing a trail of black
streaks behind as traffic wildly
zigzags to avoid Sidney blowing his
F note into the mouths of angry
commuters a glint of smog/red sun flashing
off his horn. The blackness
he leaves behind explains Kline, Rothko
& Pollock. A mail truck pulls
up beside him & tosses a letter at
Sidney contains a check from
the Ford Foundation. Sidney
stuffs the letter in his suit pocket
& plays to the departing
mail man: "These
Foolish Things
Remind me of you — Dear"

6.

the Zen Master with charge accounts
at the leading Parisian stores
comes to test Sidney in
his dressing room minutes
before his show
goes on. "Where's
your heart, my son?" Sidney
points at the bell
of his horn resting
on the creased split of his thread
bare trousers.

7.

Unlikely name for a jazz musician.
A tailor's name, shy, retiring,
"Do I have to shadowbox with
my father's ghost everytime I
sign a check?" murmurs Sidney
cashing his last.

8.

"Inner & outer confuse
me" ponders Sidney. "Inner
means: IN her & when I'm
in her my entire external
universe shrinks to walnut
size & my notes rebound sharply
off its shell & the nut meat
's as tasteless as an academic
jazz history book." Meanwhile
Sidney's reverie gets interrupted
by a Funeral Society Salesman dressed
in Mardi Gras drag. Sidney
asks for burial in a piano case
dropped into the Gulf of Mexico
"An original!" shouts the salesman
pulling out of his feathered coat
a blank policy covered with
crow's feet. Sidney signs & walks
over to the keyboard
a few drunks are lazily moaning
requests. Sidney ignores them. Plays
an A Sharp & hears the off
key piano chill his ears. Lights
a match & sets
its frame on fire. When
the police knock on the door
of his flat to arrest
him he
hears a broken
martial rhythm in their
knocking & wishes
he had remained at the club
to see if the drunks
realized
he was playing
their song

# ELEGY FOR PAUL BLACKBURN

:   the outline of an old palm
pulsing in his forehead
    's center

a great about-to-break
    skull

that I recognized
    as Paul

Blackburn's & as I was
about to ask Paul why that
        outrageous palm    a voice

behind his skull    dictated:
        "going down slow
or fast/    keep your song
    a lover's
    lament"

his lifeline pulsing
blue  like that vein next to
    the head of a cock

pulsing seconds after the act
irony: meaning: never falling out of love

    even when morning
shatters the goddamned
        windows of your skull

then there was the lush who thought
his heart as empty as a used
six pack, as

hollow,

    & above the palm writ large on
his brow:

    *25¢ KNOW YOUR FATES*

    & this time the uncontrollable
belly laughter

        was the poet's
who knew all the fates (amours) save

his own

going

down

FAST

# ODESSAN REFLECTIONS

1.

Scarlet runs from the paisley design of my grandmother's scarf into her canvas of St. George slaying the dragon. There were no dragons in her nineteenth century Odessa on the Black Sea. A resort. A retort given to the Zen addict who first told me about a painter who was terrified by the dragon he painted how it appeared to snap its fiery jaws at him sending spinal shudders so. He never painted again. Or perhaps not dragons again. I'd like to think of "dragon" as a constellation of psychosomatic sensations beginning at the crown of the skull as a tickling & racing down the back of the neck like molten lava. I had an uncle named George who was cured of a mysterious psychosomatic ailment by a Christian Science healer. My grandmother left my uncle George in the living room alone with this stranger and an hour later he was healed. He pulled the dragon out of his navel is a likely explanation. Or sent internal lava pouring from out of the brain cavity. Are there active volcanoes in Odessa? I doubt it. As for my grandmother's paisley scarf: she wasn't buried with it it must be around here somewhere.

2.

Streets full of women
dressed like gypsies. Thrill
to the music of buy
& sell. A woman will read
your cards for a kopeck. A
Holy Man from Tashkent will be
a mirror for your soul. He will strip
you of your clothes,
pretensions, manners & peer
into your soul's crevices.
You will adore being
inwardly raped by his knowing.
& loaves of stale seeded bread
to chew with each step walking home
ward with the precision
of a priest fingering
his beads.

3.

All my grandparents hailed from Odessa. Where the spring rains oppressed. I like to think of those 4 rushing home from the Marketplace with rain pelting them. The women, my grandmothers, trying weakly to maintain their dignity as their long dresses trailed in mud. Add some electrical disturbance in the air: the revolution is a decade away. When it arrives these 4 will be safely past Ellis Island & settled in Philadelphia where the likelihood of revolution in their or my lifetime is nil. An odor of ozone in the air & human sweat. The raw erotic impulse my grandfathers felt seeing the dresses of their women cling to heaving breasts. When sex occurs in 19th century Odessa it's time to bring out the priest. But in this case: the Rabbi. Give their Rabbi a Rasputin beard & insane eyes schooled in the *Zohar.* Under these cultural cliches in the real Odessa hearts broke like cannons going off in the 1812 Overture. When I think of my grandfather's lust I hear them going off & the war is over. "I can begin to live my life now" said my grandmother a week after her husband died. The rest of the family put off by her frankness. In America she found her lusting voice. In America the revolution was over before it began. She knew. She kept her fondness for Lenin to herself but when she recited Whitman she was more of a democratic socialist than either Lenin or her late husband could ever be.

4.

to hide being a jew
from Odessa is like
sewing a secret pocket
inside a pants cuff where
a coin can be stashed so
crossing the border guards
won't suspect wrongdoing. Yet

the mind with numbing regularity
hears the coin drop
at the borderguard's feet

& it was said of jews
they never easily let gold
fall out of their hands

but the guard grabs for it first
& tosses it
beyond the margin of the
forbidden border

5.

Scarf of broadcloth broad enough to carry the day's groceries back home
with. The rituals of Odessa easily transposed to early XX century Philadel-
phia. The narrow circle of men defining feminine energies. Fear in the
groin & between the eyes, a point when pressed can relieve spinal pressure.
The pressure directed toward my grandfather to leave Odessa pressing.
Didn't want to serve the Czar's will. Military refusal could be punished
by execution a noble end he refused. He fled. Not that he was a pacifist. My
grandmother can attest he was far from that pastoral climate. In Odessa a
knife in the pocket as common as a Saturday Night Special in Oakland,
California. Where Gertrude Stein found no there there. Like myself came
from Russian/Jewish stock but unlike myself primarily was homoerotic.
Odessa was no home for the Erotic. How to think in writing with images as
fragile as old photos from a family album. Digressions were endless as my
grandparents dressed in carbon black snuck over the Russian border without
papers. Each chapter of their lives fleeing Odessa out of *1001 Nights.* That
dank canvas of St. George in my grandmother's apartment reminds me of a
Knight slaying a dragon. A knight in armor & the dragon a psychosomatic
ailment. Find the Christian Scientist in the picture & what myth he fled at
night past the border guard from

6.

Strains of accordion music.
A teary run of minor mode notes.
Pipe smoke to the ceiling. The
romance of old Odessa lost forever
in a few years. In a few days my people
will pack & sever their connection
with Odessa. Except for the language. Their
crazy/quilt of Yiddish/Russian with inflections
& a vocabulary for every level
of human loss. Came to America with little
more than their skin. "Starting over"
This Odessan tale arriving in my first
year in the West "starting over" Slaying
what dragon in the nerves
finding what Odessa in my hungers
I never saw my grandmother in a scarf
She might never have owned one
but the scarlet from that scarf is the color
of my skin
I wear it knowing she died with her mind flooded with that hue
& with thoughts of the sounds
of waves from the Black Sea.

# POEMS FOR A FADING IMAGE

## 1. Religion Misunderstood Attracts False Lovers

when your exlover
at midnight, drunk, driven,
tried breaking down our
door to tell the truth
of your hours together I
should've let him in & made
peace with my demon-brother.
Instead screamed at him GO
AWAY! while you trembled a
room away

as a child asked the
Rabbi why the sterling silver
box suspended on his quivering
neck could never be opened on
penalty of sin. He spoke of God
's name written on a slip of
paper within its casing & how
no one's fit to see it.

Irony: to have opened one
secret & not the other. To pry
into God's anatomy & to leave
yours veiled. Knowing, all along,
who's the great
avenger

## 2. In Chinatown, 1967

—sitar music riding up my spine
from speakers concealed
on the ceiling—
you leaving a note on the table
after your disappearance
out the exit behind the kitchen: *we're*
*thru see you*
*in heaven* the gesture
too dramatic even
for late night buffet

## Now-That-I-Have-Followed-This-Line-To-The-End-Of-The-Earth- I-Must-Start-Over

women no longer
fandango dancers teasing
& men no longer demon-fathers
my own name a hollow mask
of many mouths
opening / closing
seeing for the first
time
how I have never seen

sacred ground to stand upon
my flesh of its matter
my heart receiving its
specific music

start over knowing

no one inhabits
the same dream
twice